Forces and Machines

KT-399-945

Contents

Introduction	2
Forces	4
How force makes things go	6
Making a windmill — *Activity*	7
Streamlined shapes	8
Poem	9
Air resistance	10
Poem	11
Stopping things — *Activities*	12
Friction	14
Poem	15
Air pressure — *Activities*	16
Air can lift	18
Flying machines	20
Poem	20
Making a glider — *Activity*	22
Making a kite — *Activity*	23
The Flying Man	24
Sir George Cayley's work with flying machines	
Compressed air — *Activities*	28
Machines	30
Poem	31
Machines in our daily lives	32
Martin the apprentice	34
Building a cathedral in the thirteenth century	
Lighter lifting	36
Cliff rescue	38
A challenge based on the pulley and the wheel and axle	
Levers, pulleys and ramps — *Activities*	40
Bank robbery!	42
Cogs, gearwheels and belts	44
A Grand Challenge!	46
Glossary and index	48

FIFE EDUCATION COMMITTEE

KING'S ROAD P. SCHOOL
ROSYTH

Introduction

What do you do when you get home from school? Make a drink perhaps? You do it by pulling open the fridge door, unscrewing the top of a bottle, lifting it up, pouring a little liquid into a glass, carrying it to the sink, turning on the tap, holding the glass carefully as it fills with water and grows heavier, turning off the tap, lifting it to your mouth and drinking. When you do something simple like making a drink, you are using forces, pressure and machines.

A force is a push or a pull and there are forces all around us. There are forces which make things go, forces which make things stop, forces which pull things down and forces which pull things up. People have force, water has force, air has force. This book concentrates, amongst other things, on the force of air: Year 6 of Ginn Science looks especially at the force of water.

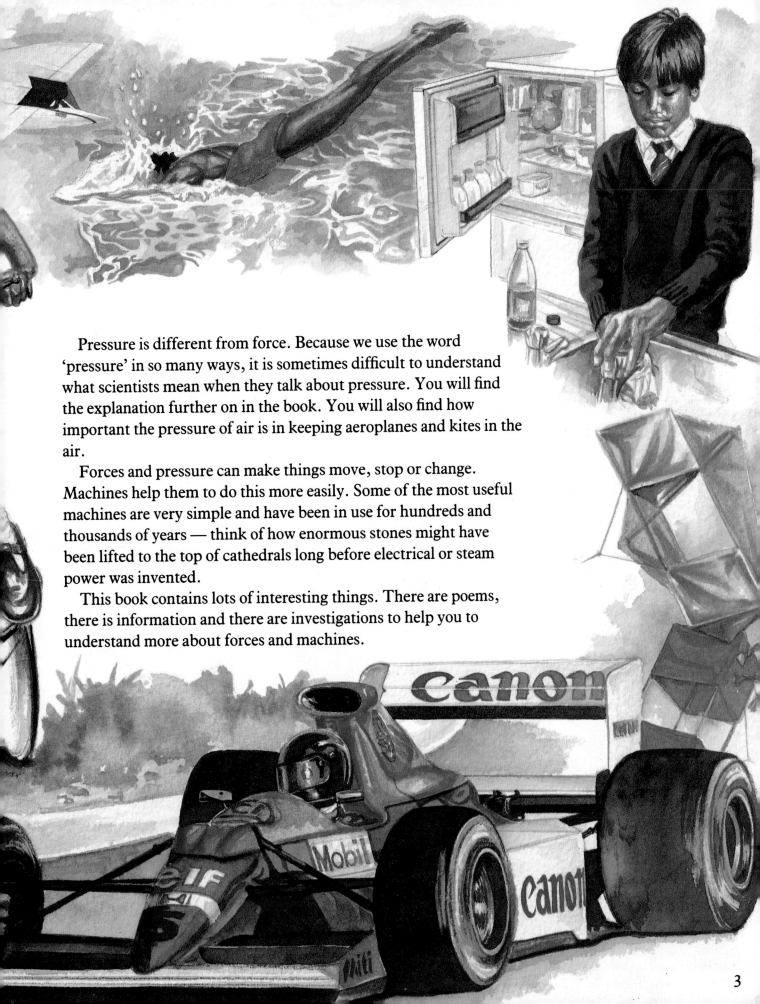

Pressure is different from force. Because we use the word 'pressure' in so many ways, it is sometimes difficult to understand what scientists mean when they talk about pressure. You will find the explanation further on in the book. You will also find how important the pressure of air is in keeping aeroplanes and kites in the air.

Forces and pressure can make things move, stop or change. Machines help them to do this more easily. Some of the most useful machines are very simple and have been in use for hundreds and thousands of years — think of how enormous stones might have been lifted to the top of cathedrals long before electrical or steam power was invented.

This book contains lots of interesting things. There are poems, there is information and there are investigations to help you to understand more about forces and machines.

Forces

Look at all the things in your classroom — the tables, the people, the books, the pencils. To make any of them move, whether they are heavy or light, some force is needed. They have to be pushed or pulled. Sometimes the force needed to move something is very gentle — such as a light puff of wind which can push a piece of paper but not a table. Sometimes the force needed is very strong — such as the force of a bulldozer which, with its powerful engine, can move huge piles of earth and stones.

Isaac Newton

Gravity

Gravity is a force that we take for granted and that we hardly think about. But it is gravity that holds things to the Earth's surface and prevents things from floating off into the atmosphere.

Isaac Newton was one of the scientists who first wrote about this force. There is a story that Isaac Newton was sitting under an apple tree in his garden when an apple fell to the ground. He wondered why it was that the apple fell downwards. Why didn't it float up into the sky? Isaac Newton realized that there is a strong force which pulls things towards the Earth, which he called gravity. We measure force in units known as newtons, named after Isaac Newton.

When you jump up into the air, your energy pushes your body off the ground but the force of gravity pulls you down again. An aeroplane needs powerful engines to launch it into the air, then the shape of the wings keeps it aloft.

There is gravity on the moon but it is much weaker than the Earth's gravity. When the American astronauts landed on the moon in 1969, they could leap and jump higher and more easily than on the Earth because the pull of gravity was less strong. The effect of the Earth's gravity gets weaker further out into space. Astronauts experience this as their spacecraft leaves the Earth's atmosphere. Slowly and gradually, the pull of the Earth's gravity becomes less strong and, as the spacecraft gets nearer the moon, the pull of the moon's gravity starts to be felt. However, the strength of the moon's **gravitational pull** is only about one sixth of the Earth's.

American astronaut climbing down from the lunar module.

How force makes things go

Moving air

We live in a world surrounded by air. We cannot see air but it presses on us and everything around us. We cannot feel still air but we can feel moving air. If you make a simple fan out of a folded piece of paper and wave it backwards and forwards in front of your face, you can feel the air moving.

We can also see the effect of moving air which can be very strong and can make other things move too. Strong trees move in the wind, even tall towers move slightly when the wind is high. The power of moving air can be trapped and controlled and used to make other things move.

For many centuries, windmills have used the power of the wind. The sails on a windmill are made from either a strong fabric like canvas, fixed on a wooden frame, or from wooden slats. The sails are attached to a mechanism that moves, so when the wind pushes against the sails, they rotate. The sail mechanism is then connected inside the mill to gearwheels which turn a great stone wheel at the bottom which grinds corn into flour.

Most traditional windmills only work when the sails point directly into the wind. Some windmills have a mechanism that makes the sails change direction as the wind changes so they always face into the wind.

Sails on boats, or sail boards, also use the push of moving air, or wind. Since the wind cannot pass through the material the sails are made of, the sails are pushed by the wind and the boat or sail board moves through the water. The sails can be adjusted to point in different directions and to face the wind at different angles. That means the boat or sail board can sail at an angle to the wind, as well as in the same direction as the wind.

Palm trees blowing in the wind

Windmill in Sussex. The smaller sails can turn the top of the windmill so that the big sails point into the wind.

The tall ships race

Racing yachts

Making a windmill

This type of windmill is one that will rotate whatever the direction of the wind. It's called the Savonius rotor.

- You can make the rotors out of an empty plastic bottle cut up.
- Fix the plastic rotors on a piece of wood or card that will spin freely. Here are some questions for you to think about.
- Does your rotor spin well when the wind blows?
- Try fixing the rotors in different positions. Which position works best?
- How can you make your test fair?
- Does the size of the rotors affect how well the machine works?
- Can you measure the speed at which your rotor spins? Can you devise a method to count the number of times it rotates in a minute?

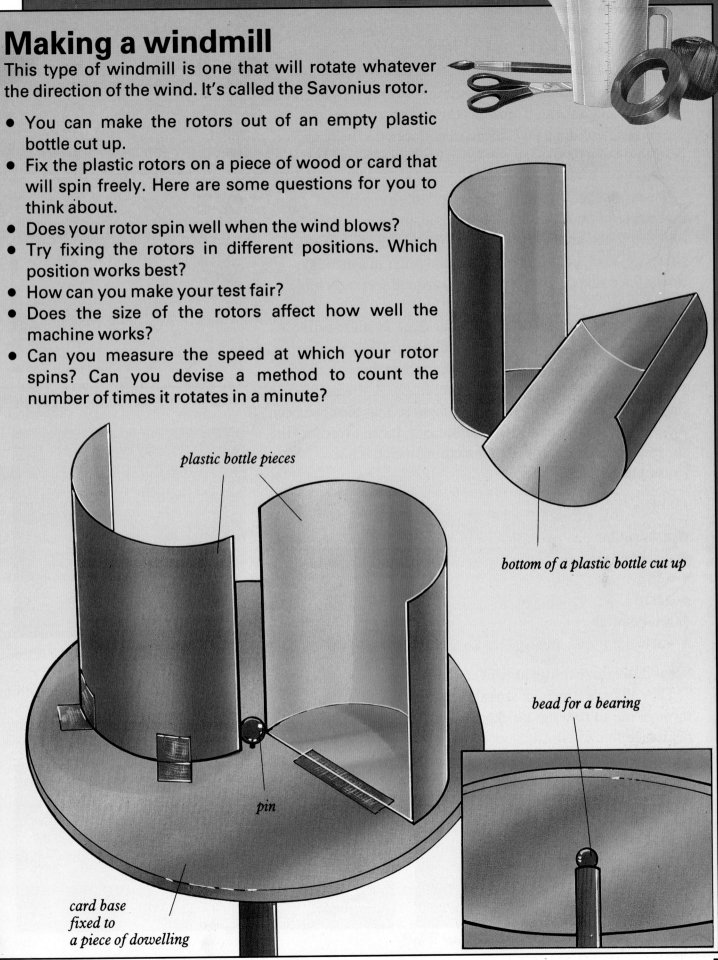

plastic bottle pieces

bottom of a plastic bottle cut up

bead for a bearing

pin

*card base
fixed to
a piece of dowelling*

Streamlined shapes

When an object travels through the air or through water, it has to push through them. Think of a time when you have tried to dive into a swimming pool and have performed a 'belly flop'. Now think of a time when you have dived into the pool successfully. Which was easier?

When you 'belly flop' into the water, more of your body hits the surface of the water at the same time, there is a loud slapping sound and it usually hurts. Whenever you perform a successful dive, your body cuts into the water in a more streamlined shape, so the water flows around you rather than against you.

Objects which travel through the air meet a similar type of resistance. A square, flat object acts like your 'belly flop'; it slaps against the air. A streamlined shape cuts through the air, allowing the air to travel round it more easily. A streamlined shape is important for speed and for flight so that the object can cut easily through the air that surrounds it. It can overcome the air resistance more easily than something which is not streamlined.

Think of the following:

- a racing car
- an aeroplane
- a fish
- a bird
- a submarine
- a seal

What do all these things have in common?

They all have streamlined shapes so that they can travel through the air or water quickly and smoothly with little resistance.

This lorry has a deflector on top of the cab to give it a more streamlined shape.

The shape of this sea-lion helps it to move quickly through the water.

Which car overcomes wind resistance best? Why?

High Dive

It feels very lonely, up here against the clouds
and girders of the glass roof. The pool so far away,
framed in flowers of a thousand upturned faces.

Walk to the brink, turn, and carefully
(firm toes gripping this last hold on life)
hang heels in space. Face a blank wall.

Raise arms slowly, sideways, shoulder-high,
silent passion, dream-deep concentration
foretelling every second of the coming flight.

Then with a sudden upward beat of palms,
of arms like wings, gathering more than thought
launch backwards into take-off, into one ball
roll for a quadruple reverse somersault
that at the last split second flicks
open like a switchblade —
feet pointed as in prayer, neat-folded hands
stab the heavens like a dagger, plunge
deep into the pool's azure flesh — without a splash.

James Kirkup

9

Air resistance

Windmills and sailing boats use the force of moving air to make them go. Other forms of transport use the force of air as a brake. Try dropping a flat sheet of paper to the ground. Watch how it floats down. Now crunch the paper into a ball and drop that from the same height. How do the two compare?

Parachutes are pulled to the ground by gravity in a similar way to the flat piece of paper. The person hanging on to the parachute falls towards the ground, but the canopy acts like a brake and stops the person from falling at breakneck speed.

The tallest parachute stack jumped successfully on 20th August 1986 in Devon. There were 24 people in the stack.

Making a parachute

Try making some parachutes from pieces of paper or cloth. Make a small parachutist out of plasticine.

- How does the weight of the parachutist affect the fall?
- How does the size of the canopy affect it?
- How does the material the canopy is made of affect it?
- Try tearing a small hole in the centre of your parachute. Does it work better?

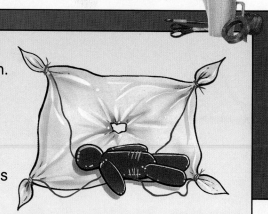

Parachute

Parachute men say
The first jump
Takes the breath away
Feet in the air disturbs
Till you get used to it

Solid ground
Is now where you left it
As you plunge down
Perhaps head first
As you listen to
Your arteries talking
You learn to sustain hope

Suddenly you are only
Holding an open umbrella
In a windy place
As the warm earth
Reaches out to you
Reassures you
The vibrating interim is over

You try to land
Where green grass yields
And carry your pack
Across the fields

The violent arrival
Puts out the joint
Earth has nowhere to go
You are at the starting point

Jumping across worlds
In condensed time
After the awkward fall
We are always at the starting point

Lenrie Peters

Stopping things

The way in which parachutes resist air can be used as a brake by machines as well as by people. Some very high speed aircraft have parachutes that open at the back when the brakes are put on. The parachutes help the aircraft slow down more quickly than the brakes alone.

A Belgian Air Force jet landing with the braking parachute flying out behind it.

Car brakes

Most cars do not need parachutes to help them stop. The brakes are good enough! The safety of a car and its passengers depends upon it having brakes that work properly. When you put on the brakes, the car does not stop immediately but takes a little time, and travels for some distance before it comes to a complete stop. That is why the driver has to leave plenty of room between her car and the one in front; she does not want to crash into the car in front. By leaving enough space between the cars, she can avoid a crash. All car drivers need to know how far their car will travel after the brakes have been put on. These distances are called 'braking distances'. The braking distance is even further on wet roads; why do you think that is?

Testing air resistance

This activity will help you feel the strength of air resistance.

- Holding an umbrella in front of you, run across the playground as fast as you can.
- Repeat the activity but this time close the umbrella before running.
- What difference can you feel to running with the umbrella open?
- Try to make your test fair by thinking about how far you run, whether there is any wind and whether you need to run in the same direction each time.

Braking distances

Distance travelled before stopping		
22.5 metres	48 kph	
52.5 metres	80 kph	
94.5 metres	112 kph	

Measure out those distances in your playground. It's a long way, isn't it?

Brakemeters

Make your own test to measure the force needed to brake a toy car.

- Using a shoe box or something similar, cut two slots, one on either side of the box.
- Push a ruler through the slots so that it will slide in and out.
- Make a ramp for the model car to run down and place the brakemeter at the bottom so that the ruler and box will stop the car from moving.
- As the car hits the ruler, the distance the ruler moves shows the force needed to stop the car.
- Conduct different tests so that the car is travelling at different speeds.
- Do cars of different weights have different braking distances?
- Does the surface of the slope affect the braking distance?
- Fasten a small doll to the car. What happens to the doll when the car hits the box?

Friction

What kinds of things do you do when you are cold? Stamp your feet? Wave your arms? Rub your hands together?

Rubbing your hands together quickly makes them warmer. This is because of a force known as friction. When two surfaces are together they 'stick' and this sticking force is called friction. Some surfaces don't 'stick' very much and move easily over each other. They don't have a lot of friction. Other surfaces do 'stick' and are hard to move over each other. They have a lot of friction.

When we run fast the friction between our feet and the ground helps us to run faster. Which kind of race would you prefer to run in, one where you run on wet grass wearing slippery shoes or one on an asphalt track wearing good trainers? Can you explain why?

Why do you think it is difficult to walk on icy pavements or on a highly polished floor? What do these surfaces have in common?

Try rubbing different surfaces together to see whether they have a lot of friction, or only a little.

Measuring the force needed to pull a brick
Make a fair test to measure the force needed to pull a brick along different surfaces. Use these things to help you:

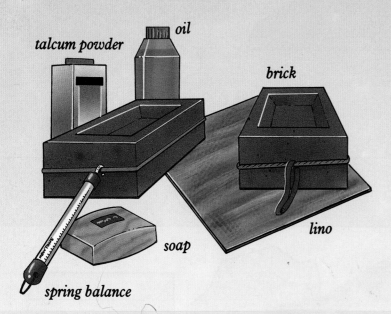

talcum powder

oil

brick

spring balance

soap

lino

What can you say about the friction that each of the different surfaces has?

Does changing the surface the brick is on, or putting something under the brick, change the amount of force needed to pull it? Try tying a duster or a soft cloth round the brick. Try using some of these:

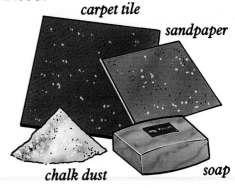

carpet tile

sandpaper

chalk dust

soap

Which of these help **lubricate** the surfaces?

Skating on Thin Lino

Because there is no Ice Rink
Within fifty miles of our house,
My sister perfects her dance routines
In the Olympic Stadium of my bedroom.
Wearing a soft expression
And two big, yellow dusters on her feet,
She explodes out of cupboards
To an avalanche of music
And whirls about the polished lino
In a blur of double axles and triple salkoes.
For her free style doubles
She hurls this pillow called Torvill
From here to breakfast time
While spinning like a drunken hippo
Round and round my bed.
Imagine waking up to that each morning!
Small wonder my hands shake
And I'm off my cornflakes.
Last Thursday she even made me
Stand up on my bed
And hold up cards marked 'Six'
While she gave endless victory salutes
In the direction of the gerbil's cage.
To be honest,
Despite her practice and her endless dedication,
I don't think she has a hope
Of lifting the world title.
But who cares;
She may not get the gold
But I bet there isn't another skater alive
With wall to wall mirror
On her bedroom floor.

Gareth Owen

15

Air pressure

Air streams

- Try blowing out a candle with an obstacle between you and the candle.
- Fix a sheet of card in front of the candle and blow against the card.
- What happens to the flame?
- Put a drinks can in front of the flame and blow against the can.
- What happens to the flame now?

What can you say about how air travels around, or is stopped by, different shaped objects? Try the same activity with some more objects. Can you predict what will happen each time?

Make sure that the card is a safe distance from the candle and do not leave this activity unattended.

Lifting paper

Air that moves does not have as much sideways push as air that is still.

- Cut a strip of paper.
- Hold the paper just under your bottom lip.
- Now blow steadily over the paper.
- What happens?

When you blow over the paper, you are moving the air above it and so you are reducing the air's pushing power. The pushing power of the air under the paper remains the same.

Breaking wood

- Take a thin strip of wood about 15 cm long or an old wooden ruler.
- Place it on a desk so that about 5 cm sticks out over the edge.
- Put a folded sheet of newspaper over the part of the ruler that is on the desk.
- Hit the other end of the ruler sharply.
- What happens?
- Now open up the sheet of newspaper and smooth it flat out over the ruler and the desk. The newspaper must be flat against the desk with no air underneath it.
- Hit the end of the ruler again.
- What happens this time?

A similar activity appears in 'Earth and Weather' on page 17. Can you see the connection?

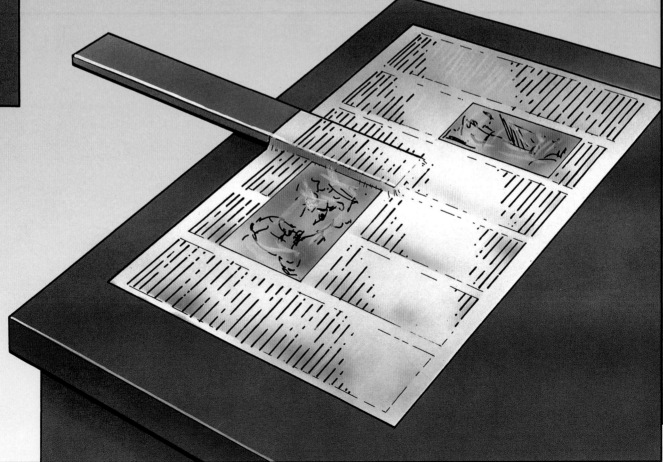

Air can lift

A streamlined shape, such as the body of a bird or an aeroplane, is necessary for flight but the shape of the wing is also very important. It is designed to use the air's push to give it what we call **lift**.

The wing of a bird or an aeroplane is shaped so that it is curved on the top and flat underneath. Although the movement of birds and aeroplanes through the air is quite complicated, you can demonstrate in the classroom what happens when the wings pass through the air as a bird glides or an aeroplane flies.

Arrange some chairs in the shape of a wing so that one surface is curved and the other is straight like this:

Concorde

Making an aerofoil

- Take a piece of A4 paper and tape the two edges together, without creasing the paper, so that the paper makes a wing shape. This is an aerofoil.
- Gently push a knitting needle through the centre of the aerofoil so that a small hole is made in each side.
- Push a straw through the holes.
- Thread a piece of cotton through the straw and tie a pencil to each end.
- Now move your aerofoil quickly but steadily through the air, or hold it in a current of air from a hair dryer. What happens?

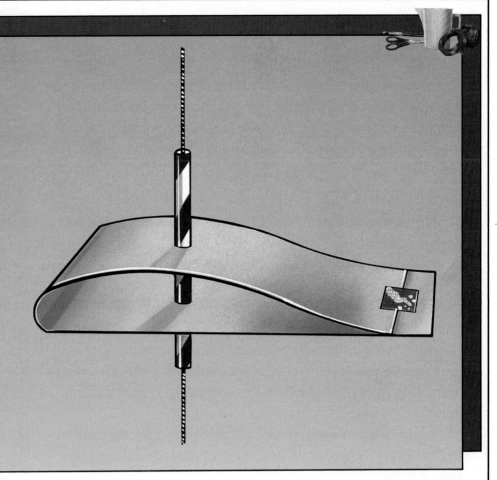

Ask a group of children to line up in pairs, one on either side of the 'wing' and to walk to the other end. Each child must try to arrive at the other end of the wing at the same time as the corresponding child on the other side. What happened to the children as they walked along the wing? Did they all walk at the same speed or did some have to go faster? Which side had to move faster to keep the line straight? Try this a few times and watch carefully to see what happens.

Measure the curved edge of the 'wing' and compare it with the length of the straight edge. Which is longer? Does that help you explain why some children had to walk faster to keep the edge straight?

In this experiment, the children played the part of the air, and the chairs were arranged like the wing. In real flight, air has further to travel over the curved top of the wing so it travels faster than the air moving under the wing. The air that travels faster has less push. The wing is held up by the greater push of the air underneath the wing.

Flying machines

For many centuries, scientists and inventors studied birds in flight and wondered whether it would be possible for humans to join the birds flying high up in the air. Many people believed that flying machines would look like birds, with wings that flapped.

Kites

Kites were the first flying objects made by humans and were made in China over 2000 years ago. Today, kites are used for all kinds of purposes — for pleasure, for crop spraying and even to carry radio-controlled cameras.

A kite flies by trapping air under its wings as it is held by its line. Fast-moving air flows over the top of the kite, while the slower-moving air under the wings pushes upwards. The line of the kite controls its movement. The pull of the line, the weight of the kite and the push of the air combine to keep the kite in flight.

This is why you need to run, or have quite a strong wind to launch a small kite. It needs moving air to create enough push to help it to fly.

In the 1800s, people began to experiment to find a kite that could carry a man. In 1901, Samuel Cody designed several kites which, together, could lift and hold a man in the air. This kind of experiment was important at this time because it helped in the study of aircraft.

Samuel Cody and (right) one of his kites

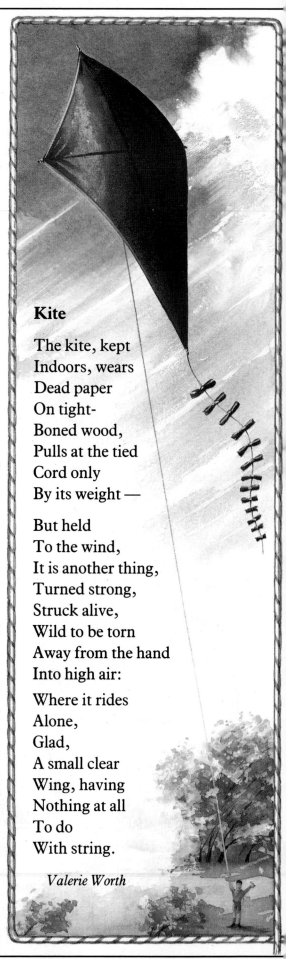

Kite

The kite, kept
Indoors, wears
Dead paper
On tight-
Boned wood,
Pulls at the tied
Cord only
By its weight —

But held
To the wind,
It is another thing,
Turned strong,
Struck alive,
Wild to be torn
Away from the hand
Into high air:

Where it rides
Alone,
Glad,
A small clear
Wing, having
Nothing at all
To do
With string.

Valerie Worth

Gliders

Most gliders fly without engines or motors to power them. They are pulled up into the sky by small powered aircraft and then released at a certain height. Some gliders do have very small engines so that they can take off without the help of another aircraft. The long wings of the gliders give them good lift and their light bodies mean that there is less pull downwards towards the ground. Gliders can stay aloft for a long time, especially if they catch a thermal. A thermal is a current of warm air that rises. A glider can use the rising warm air to give it extra lift. Many birds use thermals in a similar way. You may have seen seagulls soaring upwards like this, apparently making no effort.

During the last century, many people tried to make flying machines. Some people made gliders that would stay in the air for a distance of only a few feet. One such man was Otto Lilienthal who lived in Germany. He made gliders which had two wings, attached by a crossbar. Otto would take a glider to the top of a hill near his home and run down the hill holding it, by the crossbar, above his head. It was very hard work. When he felt the air catch the wings, he would lift his feet and remain airborne for a few seconds.

Otto Lilienthal made many successful gliding flights. The only thing that was holding him back was that he did not have an engine that was light but powerful enough to push his glider into the air.

The breakthrough in flight happened at the beginning of this century when Orville and Wilbur Wright managed a short, but successful, powered flight.

Otto Lilienthal in one of his gliders.

The first flight in a powered aeroplane, achieved in 1903 by the Wright brothers.

Making a glider

Can you fold a piece of stiff paper into a glider that flies well? These diagrams will help you make a simple paper glider. See how you can change the way it flies by adding paper-clips or plasticine to parts of it, or by folding the wing flaps.

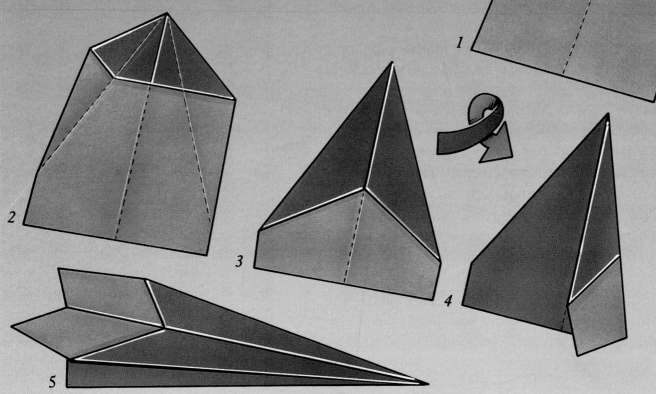

1

2

3

4

5

- Whose glider flies best? (You'll need to discuss what you mean by 'best'.)
- Whose glider flies furthest in a straight line? (You'll need to decide on a fair way to launch the gliders. Perhaps you could make a mechanical launcher, using elastic bands, some wood and a ruler.)
- Can you make a glider that loops the loop?
- Whose glider stays in the air for the longest time?

Can you make a larger glider, with a body and wings, using stiff paper, sticky tape or glue and some thin wood? Your glider must have a wing span of at least 50 cm.

Whose is the best glider? What qualities do you look for to judge which is the best?

The world record for the longest flight of a paper aeroplane is just under 17 seconds. It was achieved by Ken Blackburn in America on 29th November 1983.

The largest flying paper aeroplane was made at the Old Warden Aerodrome in Bedfordshire on 26th April 1986 by Grahame Foster, David Broom and Andrew Barnes. It was launched from a platform just over 3 m high and flew nearly 16.5 m.

Making a kite

- You will need a sheet of newspaper or some large sheets of tissue-paper, some long pieces of cane, dowelling or art straws, some paper for the tail, a lot of thin string and an old wooden ruler.

- Fasten two pieces of rod together like this. The long rod going downwards should be twice the length of the rod that goes across.

- Cut a piece of paper in a diamond shape like this and fix it to the rods with sticky tape. You may need to make an edge of thin string or rods to fix the paper to.

- Make a tail by tying a long piece of string round pieces of paper or cloth and then tie it to the bottom of the kite.

- Attach strings to the four corners of the kite and tie them together where they cross in the middle. Fix a long piece of string to the cross-pieces and tie the ruler on as a handle.

- Now try to fly your kite. Are there any ways you can improve it?

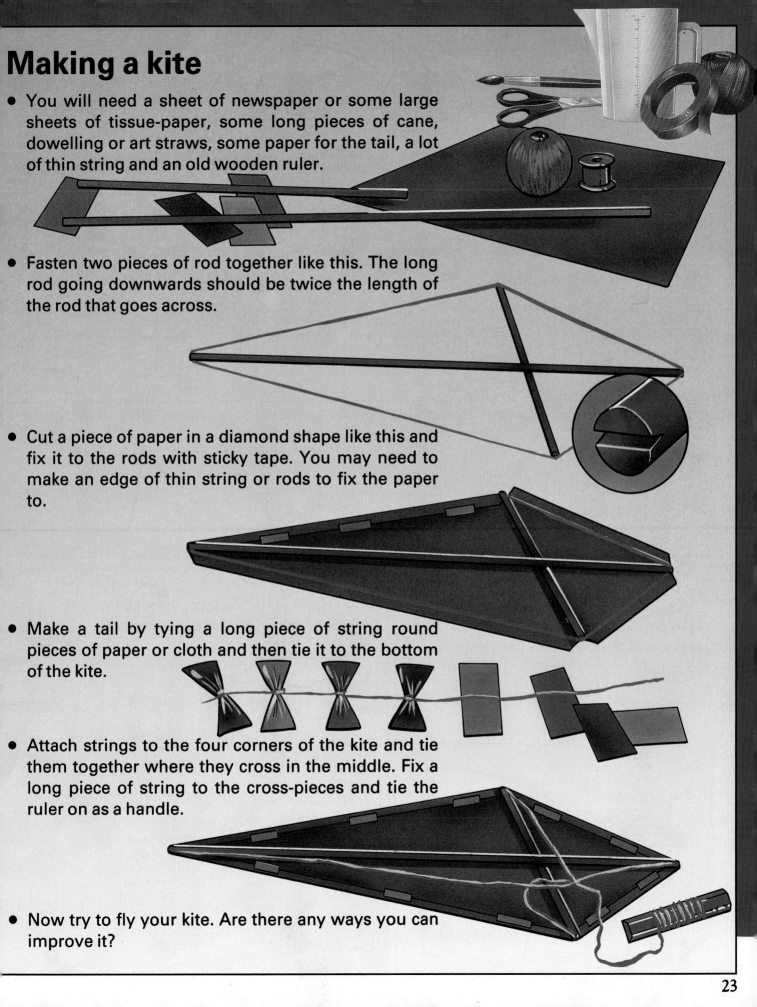

The Flying Man

Two hundred years ago, when George Cayley was a boy, aeroplanes had not been invented. If people wanted to visit other countries they had to go by ship.

1 Cayley wanted to invent a way in which human beings could fly. He studied birds very carefully, sketching them as they flew and he made scientific drawings. He drew the birds' wing shapes. He drew their tails and he made careful notes.

If humans are going to fly, I must get this right.

2 The first flying machine that Cayley built was like a boat, with wings instead of oars. You sat in it and flapped the wings. Cayley hoped that the flapping would lift the machine into the air, as wings lift birds.

G. Cayley, Esq.

3 He tried it one afternoon, in a field beside the house. He sat in the machine, flapping the wings. It was hard work. He puffed and sweated.

That's a silly idea. That thing won't fly.

4 Cayley went back to his desk. He looked again at his drawings of birds. He worked out what was wrong. Birds have powerful wings and strong chest muscles which flap them. Human arms and chests are quite different. They don't have enough power to lift a flying machine into the air.

No more flapping. Fixed wings will be better. The machine should be able to glide and soar.

5 Nowadays, we know that Cayley was right and successful aeroplanes have fixed wings. But Cayley was the first person to think of it. He drew wings of all shapes — circles, diamonds, triangles, squares — and he made card and wooden models and tested them.

6 His tests took years. Every day, Cayley wrote in his study or flew models in the fields. Each time the models crashed, he went home to think about what had gone wrong and what improvements he could make.

He'll never do it. Humans aren't built to fly. Leave flying to the birds.

7 Cayley's work showed him that the best wing shape was a long rectangle shaped like a ruler. He made wings big enough to carry the weight of a dog. Each wing was 1.5 metres long. The wings were made of wood and cloth. Cayley tied a basket to the wings and put the dog in it. Then he launched the model from a small hill into the wind and watched it fly.

8 The dog-in-the-basket flew safely down to the field. The dog peered over the side of the basket.

He's crazy!

That's very good!

25

9 After the dog-flight, Cayley wrote a book that explained how moving currents of air help birds to fly. But, for a while, he stopped his experiments with flying machines. He wanted to do other scientific work. He built a telescope and began star-gazing. He also designed artificial arms and legs for people in the local hospital.

10 Forty years went by, until Cayley was an old man, a great-grandfather. In all that time, no one else had built a successful flying machine. Inventors made railways and steamships. No one bothered with the sky.

11 Cayley decided to continue his work with flying machines. This time, he built a glider big enough to carry a human being. His coachman, John Appleby, helped him. When the machine was ready, Cayley sent for a boy from the village. Cayley gave him sixpence and asked him to sit in the glider. The boy had no idea what was in store. He did as Cayley asked.

12 Then Cayley and Appleby heaved the glider into the air from the top of a hill. It flew for ten seconds before bumping to the ground. The boy spilled out, howling with terror.

13 John Appleby was glad too soon. Cayley's next machine was big enough for a grown man. Six farm-hands carried it to the hillside and set it up. Cayley took Appleby's arm and coaxed him to sit inside. His white hair blew in the wind.

14 Unwillingly, Appleby sat down. The men pushed the glider down the hill. It rose in the air, flew for 500 metres, bumped on the ground and stopped.

15 Appleby crawled out, terrified. He shook his fist, and walked away, never wanting to see Cayley or his flying machines again. Without realizing it, he had taken part in one of science's most exciting advances.

Compressed air

Air can be squashed. When you pump up a bicycle tyre, you are squashing the air in it so that more air can be squeezed in. Squashed air is called compressed air. Bicycle tyres can be pumped so full of compressed air that they feel very hard. Compressed air is very strong. Car tyres have to be filled with compressed air too, otherwise they do not support the weight of the car and the tyres go flat.

Lifting weights with compressed air
- Put a balloon on a table so that the end of the balloon is jutting over the edge.
- Put some books on to the balloon.
- Now blow up the balloon.
- What happens?

Making a jet-propelled balloon
- Blow up a balloon then attach it to a straw with sticky tape.
- Thread the straw on to some taut string or wire suspended across the classroom.
- Untie the balloon and let go of it.
- What happens?
- How could you improve your jet?

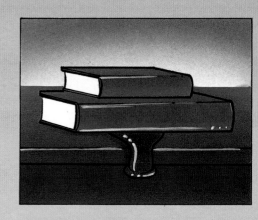

drinking straw

string

Making a hovercraft

This hovercraft is quite tricky to make but it is successful if you make sure there are no holes that might leak air.

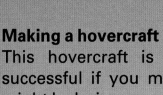

- Roll up a piece of card so that it will fit tightly into the neck of a balloon.
- Glue one end of the card tube to a paper plate and make a tiny pin-hole in the part of the plate covered by the card tube.
- Blow up a balloon, as much as you can, and put one end of the card roll into the neck of the balloon. Try not to let any air escape. You may need a friend to help you.
- Put the whole thing on to a smooth surface and let go.
- The air should escape from the balloon, down through the hole, and push the plate just off the surface like a hovercraft.

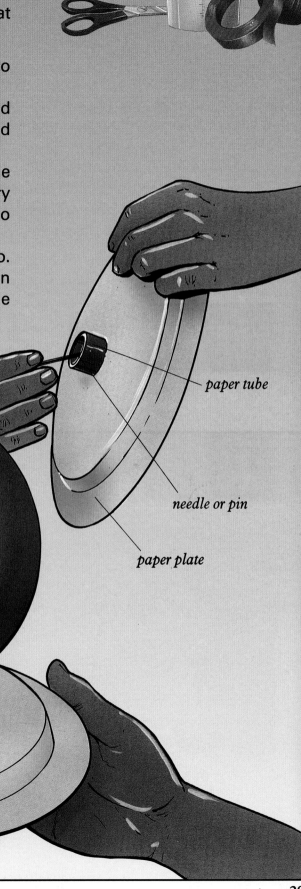

paper tube

needle or pin

paper plate

Machines

Machines are built to help us with our work and to make things easier for us. They use different forces and they can increase the work that the forces can do. When we use the word 'machine', we usually think of a factory machine, a computer or a washing-machine. In fact, most machines are very simple. When scientists talk about machines, they can mean five simple devices that don't look machine-like at all. Yet these five basic machines are vital for any mechanical device to work!

This page is a spotting game. On it, you will find some examples of the five simple machines. Read the descriptions carefully; then look at the garage, and see how many you can spot!

The secret of the machines

We were taken from the ore-bed and the mine,
    We were melted in the furnace and the pit —
We were cast and wrought and hammered to design,
    We were cut and filed and tooled and gauged to fit.
Some water, coal, and oil is all we ask.
    And a thousandth of an inch to give us play:
And now, if you will set us to our task,
    We will serve you four and twenty hours a day!

    We can pull and haul and push and lift and drive,
    We can print and plough and weave and heat and light,
    We can run and race and swim and fly and dive,
    We can see and hear and count and read and write!

Rudyard Kipling

The easiest machine to spot is the **wheel and axle**. We see hundreds every day. Just how many wheels can you spot in this picture? Another form of the wheel is one which has 'teeth' which will interlock with another. Each tooth is known as a cog.

The **pulley** helps us to lift heavy things straight up. All you need for a pulley is a fixed point over which you can put a rope. Most pulleys, though, are more complicated than a rope slung over something.

The simplest kind of machine is the **lever**. A lever is a rod or bar which moves on a fixed point. The fixed point is called the fulcrum, or the **pivot**. A pair of scales is a lever, with the balance point as the pivot. So is a wheelbarrow, where the centre of the wheel is the pivot. Levers are very useful when you want to move a heavy load or move something stiff. You may have used one when you opened a paint tin with a spoon.

Another simple machine is the **ramp**. You might call it a slope. You can see ramps in many places. They may not look much like machines but ramps help us to lift heavy things.

We use **screws** in lots of different ways — to lift loads, to join things strongly with nuts and bolts and to put tops on bottles.

Machines in our daily lives

Examples of the five basic machines — the pulley, the wheel and axle, the lever, the ramp and the screw — are all round us in our environment. We use these types of machines every day. In fact, simple household tools are machines.

What kind of machines are these common tools?

Designing helpful tools

- Re-design an everyday household tool so that it can be used by someone who has difficulty gripping.
- Think of an everyday tool which might be difficult to grip.
- What is it about this tool that causes the difficulty?
- What can be done to overcome this difficulty?
- Try to design a way of overcoming the difficulty.
- Now make your tool and test it.
- Can you think of any way you could make it better?

indoor washing line

tap

SYRUP

FLOUR

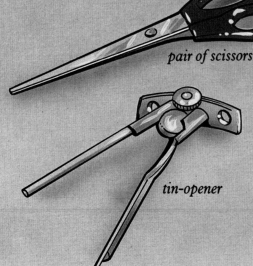

pair of scissors

spoon

tin-opener

BEANS

corkscrew

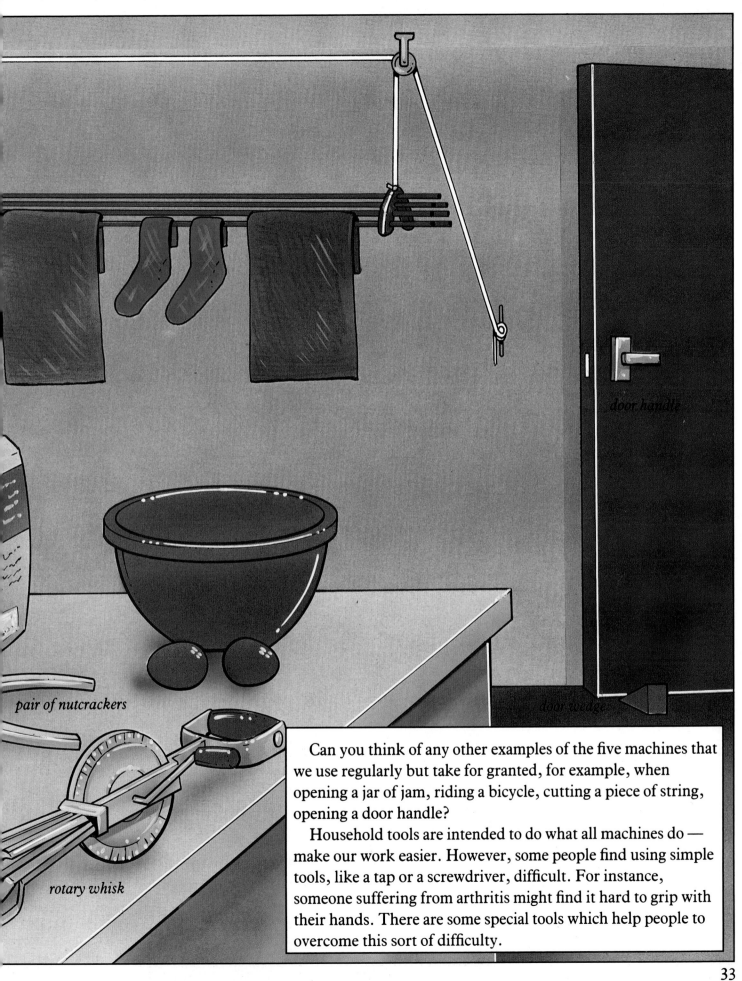

door handle

pair of nutcrackers

door wedge

rotary whisk

Can you think of any other examples of the five machines that we use regularly but take for granted, for example, when opening a jar of jam, riding a bicycle, cutting a piece of string, opening a door handle?

Household tools are intended to do what all machines do — make our work easier. However, some people find using simple tools, like a tap or a screwdriver, difficult. For instance, someone suffering from arthritis might find it hard to grip with their hands. There are some special tools which help people to overcome this sort of difficulty.

artin the apprentice

My name is Martin. I am one of the **apprentices** to Peter, who is the master **mason** for the building of our new cathedral.

I am thirteen years of age. I was born in 1250, ten years after work began on the cathedral.

I remember well the day that my mother apprenticed me to the master mason. It is a good apprenticeship. I hope that one day I will be a master mason myself.

But first, I have to do the simple jobs. The dull jobs. The jobs that nobody else wants to do. It is all part of learning to be a mason.

1 When I first arrived, Peter showed me a great roof beam, as thick as a man's arm, and as long as my father is tall. "Now then, young Martin," said Peter, "the carpenters want this beam in the roof, double quick. Take it up to them, will you?"

2 Well, I looked up at all the dizzying ladders and wondered how I was to do it. But I was determined, so I put my hands under the beam and heaved. Of course, I couldn't lift it. Peter himself could not have lifted it. Then I noticed the men laughing — not unkindly. It was a trick, and I had been caught.

3 "Nay, Martin. It is easier to pull down than lift up!" And Peter took me to a rope, which was slung over a wheel fixed high in the cathedral roof. In a few moments, he fastened the beam safely to the rope. Peter gave me the other end of the rope. "Now pull, young Martin! And the pulley will do the work!"

4 I hauled on the rope. It was magical. The beam rose into the air as if it were a splinter. After that, I spent many hours working with the pulley. I learned to let the rope and wheel do the work, and surprised myself — and the other apprentices — with the loads I could raise up into the roof.

5 One morning, some weeks later, I found a team of men busy with my pulley. They were preparing to lift a huge wooden wheel into the rafters of the cathedral. "Now, Martin," said Peter, "it is time that the masons lifted their great stones into the sky. Even you could not lift them with the pulley alone. We must use the great wheel!"

It took all morning but at last the great wooden wheel was mounted in the roof of the cathedral, turning on a thick wooden shaft. A heavy rope was round about the shaft, and hung to the ground. "Are you much of a walker, Martin?" said Peter. "Yes, Sir," I answered.

6 It was as well. I was to walk miles over the next few weeks, walking round inside the great wheel, and pulling the rope up into the heights of the cathedral. On the rope were stones many times my own weight; but the great wheel made them easy to lift — as long as I was prepared to walk a long way! My strides inside the wheel made the wheel and the great shaft turn and pull up the rope.

7 Time has passed, and younger, newer apprentices than me now walk the great wheel. But I still find it fascinating how a person can lift such heavy loads with the help of that one wheel!

35

Lighter lifting

The first person to throw a vine over a tree branch and haul a weight into the air had discovered a simple machine — the pulley. The pulley works because it is easier to pull down than to lift up.

But vines — and ropes — rub on branches, and make the lifting harder. They can fray and break. It is much easier to put the rope through a fixed wheel. To be accurate, it is this wheel, and not the rope, that scientists and engineers call a pulley.

If the wheel is grooved, that prevents the rope slipping out. And if the pulley wheel is oiled and greased, it will turn much more easily. A dry, squeaky pulley wheel is hard work!

A fixed pulley wheel and a moving one can make a heavy load seem far lighter; but you have to pull the rope a lot further than with a single pulley! Can you see how much further the rope will have to be pulled to lift the load a short distance?

The more wheels you add to the pulley system, the longer the rope you need — and the heavier the load that the pulley can lift. The pulley wheels are mounted in groups known as 'blocks'. A system of pulleys and ropes is called a block and tackle. With a block and tackle, work is made easier and one person can lift a car engine.

All machines make work easier. Without pulleys, we would find it much harder to lift and move heavy things. But all pulleys must be kept well lubricated, or we use all our effort in overcoming friction!

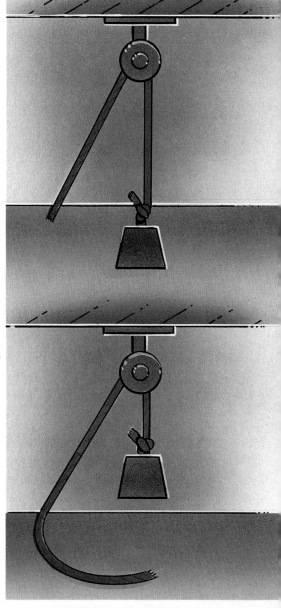

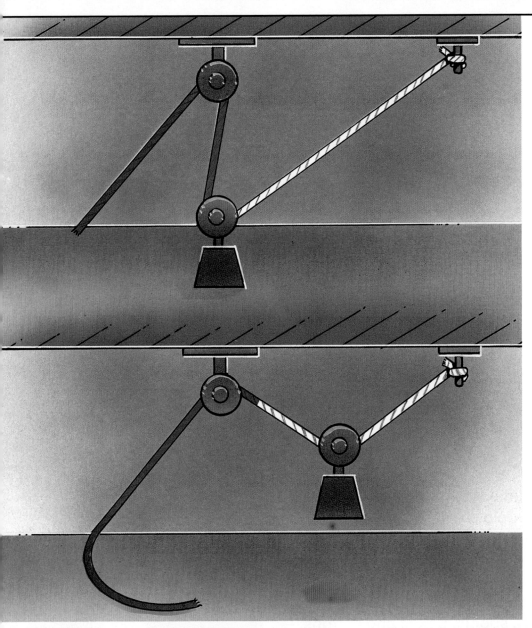

Double pulley
A double pulley lifts a weight a short distance for a long pull on the rope; but the load feels lighter.

Cliff rescue

Emergency! Karen and Mark have climbed down the cliff face to explore a secret bay. But while their backs were turned, the tide has come in, trapping them. There is no time to call the coastguard boat, or summon a helicopter. You have to rescue them; AND get them to a doctor as both are suffering from cold and shock. Can you do it? You have sixty minutes before the tide comes in.

- Your table top is the cliff edge.
- Two dolls or model people are Karen and Mark.
- The floor is the shore.
- You can use a construction kit or alternatively you can use a range of building materials — thin wood, lolly sticks, card, glue and string. Some junk materials — card rolls, spools, boxes and cartons — might be useful too.
- You must get Karen and Mark up the cliff, and transport them to a doctor.
- One machine can do both jobs but it might be quicker if your group worked on two machines.
- You can send a rescuer down to Karen and Mark — for example, you can pretend that one of you goes down to tie a rope around their waist — but you must get that rescuer back.
- You can't, of course, glue or pin things to the table. Ask your teacher if you can use sticky tape to keep your machine still. You have sixty minutes before the tide comes in.

Good luck! Karen and Mark are depending on you.

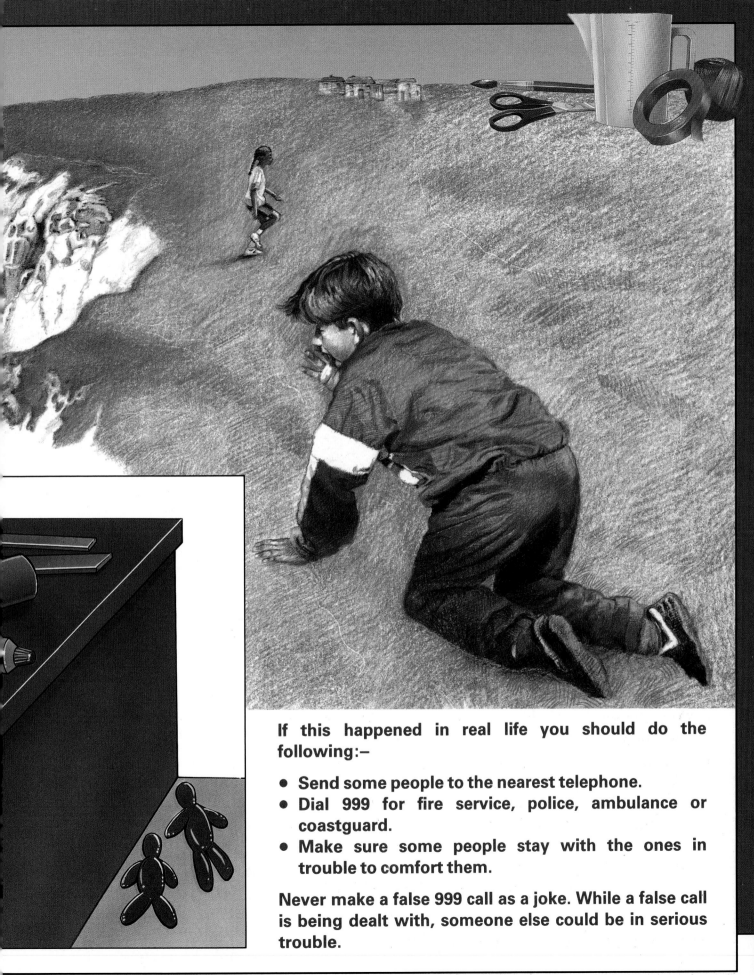

If this happened in real life you should do the following:–

- Send some people to the nearest telephone.
- Dial 999 for fire service, police, ambulance or coastguard.
- Make sure some people stay with the ones in trouble to comfort them.

Never make a false 999 call as a joke. While a false call is being dealt with, someone else could be in serious trouble.

Levers, pulleys and ramps

Investigating levers

- Take an empty syrup or paint tin and try using different objects to remove the lid. Which works best?

Investigating pulleys

- Tie a piece of string round a brick.
- Try lifting the brick.
- Now fix a cotton reel to something solid so that you can use it as a pulley wheel to help you lift the brick.
- Can you devise a fair test to measure the force needed to lift the brick with and without the pulley wheel?
- What effect does using two pulley wheels have?

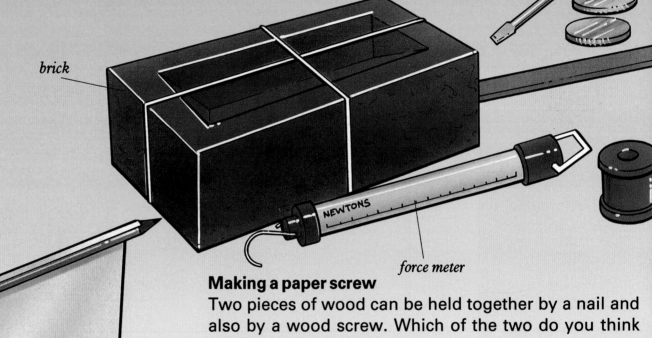

brick

force meter

Making a paper screw

Two pieces of wood can be held together by a nail and also by a wood screw. Which of the two do you think would be stronger? Why?

A screw is a very simple machine that is linked closely with the ramp.

- Take a rectangular piece of paper measuring 15 cm × 30 cm.
- Cut the paper into two along the diagonal.
- Wrap the paper around a pencil, rolling so that the 30 cm side forms the base of the triangle. Keep this edge straight.
- Your paper should now look like a screw.

Investigating ramps

- Lift a wood block on to the top of a ramp, made from a piece of hardboard and some blocks, using a force meter.
- Measure the force needed to lift the block to the top of the ramp.
- Place the block at the bottom of the ramp and measure the force needed to drag it up the ramp to the top.
- Try using a longer slope but the same height. Does this make any difference?
- Does changing the surface of the ramp make any difference?
- Does putting dowel rollers under the block make any difference?

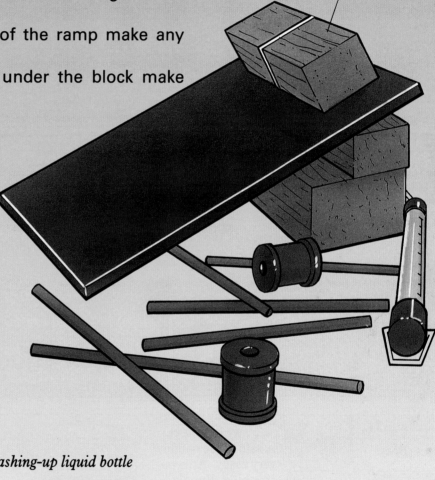

wood block

paper clip

elastic band

washing-up liquid bottle

bead as a bearing

Climbing a ramp

- Make a washing-up liquid racer using a plastic bottle and elastic bands. You may have already made one in Year 3.
- Can you make the 'racer' climb a ramp?
- How can you improve its grip?
- What is the steepest slope that your racer will climb?
- Can your racer carry a load to the top of the ramp? How heavy can the load be? Does the amount of slope affect how heavy the load can be?

Bank robbery!

There, Bungle, there! In that safe there is enough money to make me, I mean us, rich for the rest of our lives!

But, Boss, how are we going to get it open? We've no dynamite.

Open it, Bungle? Open it? We're not going to open it. We're going to steal it, contents and all. Then we'll open it at our leisure. Now, quickly, lift it with your lever! Over the pivot, so!

1

Now for my master plan. With the simple application of the wheel and axle . . .

2

. . . and the addition of the slope or ramp . . .

3

Oh, yes, Boss!

. . . we can move the safe to the window very easily. Are you pushing, Bungle?

4

Can you move the safe?
- Try moving your own 'safe' in the same way as Bungle and Boss.
- Use a brick as the 'safe' and place it on a table, inside a box.
- Using a lever, wheel and axle, ramp and pulley, remove the brick from the box and lower it to the floor.

Cogs, gearwheels and belts

Looking at cogs and gears

A gearwheel is a wheel which has teeth around the rim. We call these teeth cogs. When gearwheels are put together so that their cogs interlock, the turn of one gearwheel will **drive** the other. This arrangement of gearwheels is called a gear.

- Look carefully at the gearwheel which is attached to the pedals on a bicycle. If you turn the pedal once, how many times does the gearwheel turn and how many times does the back wheel turn?
- Can you see why this happens?

Making gearwheels and gears

- Cut twelve ice-lolly sticks in half and stick the two halves of each lolly stick together.
- Cut out four cardboard circles of the same size.
- Place two of the circles flat on your desk and arrange the lolly sticks across them as in the picture.
- Glue the lolly sticks on to the card circles and then glue the other two circles on top of the sticks. You have now made two gearwheels.
- Fasten the circles to a board using drawing pins which will act as axles allowing the circles to move.
- Mesh the gearwheels together so that the cogs can work on each other.
- What happens when you turn one wheel?

Make some gearwheels of different sizes.

- Can you make an arrangement of two different-sized gearwheels so that one turn of one gearwheel makes the other gearwheel turn twice?
- Can you arrange the gearwheels so that you can turn an upwards/downwards movement into an across movement?
- What happens if you try three gearwheels together?

By changing from one size gearwheel to another with a different number of cogs, you can slow down or increase the speed at which the same wheel will turn. This is known as 'changing gear'.

ice-lolly sticks

card circ

Belts

You can also drive one wheel with another by using a belt. The belt loops around the two wheels. One wheel has to have a source of power which will turn it. The belt then sends or transmits this power to the other wheel, making it turn. This is called a belt drive. You may have made simple belts in Year 3 of Ginn Science, using two cotton reels and an elastic band.

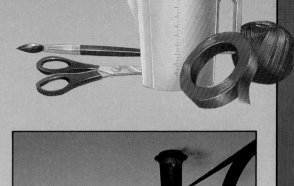

Making belts

- Try making a belt drive using two different-sized wheels, e.g. a cotton reel and a coffee jar lid.
- What effect does this have?
- Does it make any difference if the driver wheel is larger or smaller?
- What happens if the belt is crossed in a figure of eight?

Belts are used in washing-machines, food mixers, vacuum cleaners and sewing-machines. But belts can slip, so they are often grooved or notched to give a firmer grip. A row of connected links — a chain — can give even more grip, especially on a toothed wheel.

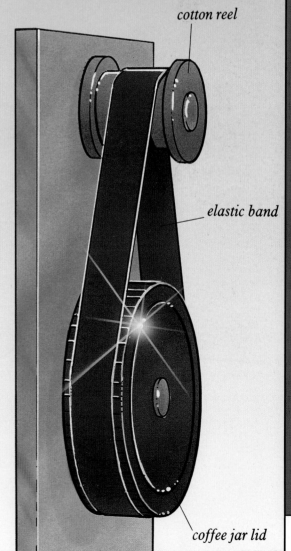

cotton reel

elastic band

coffee jar lid

A Grand Challenge!

Make a game or toy using at least two of the simple machines that we have looked at in this book. Here are some suggestions:

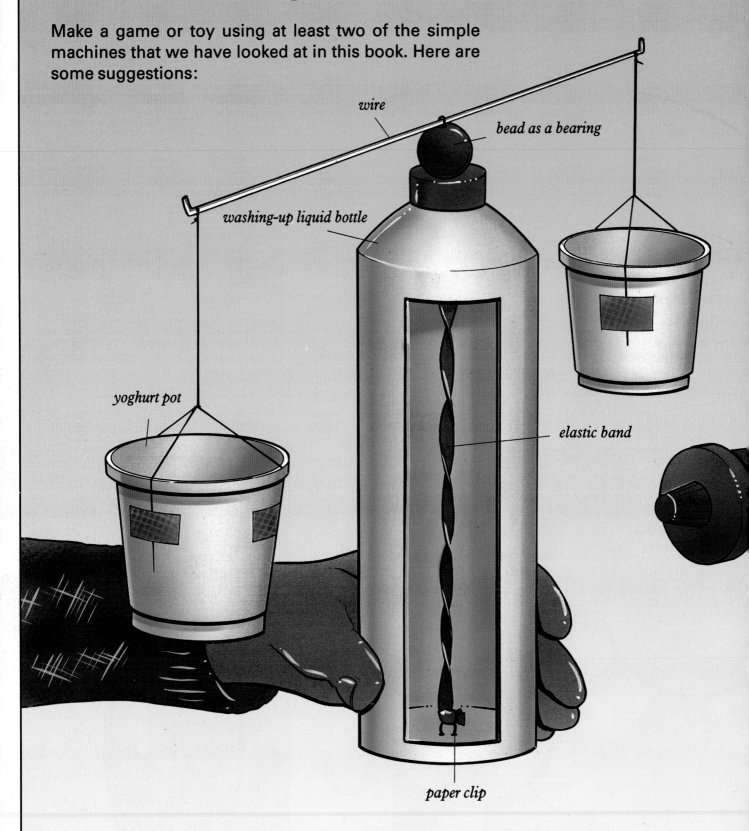

wire

bead as a bearing

washing-up liquid bottle

yoghurt pot

elastic band

paper clip

A fairground carousel

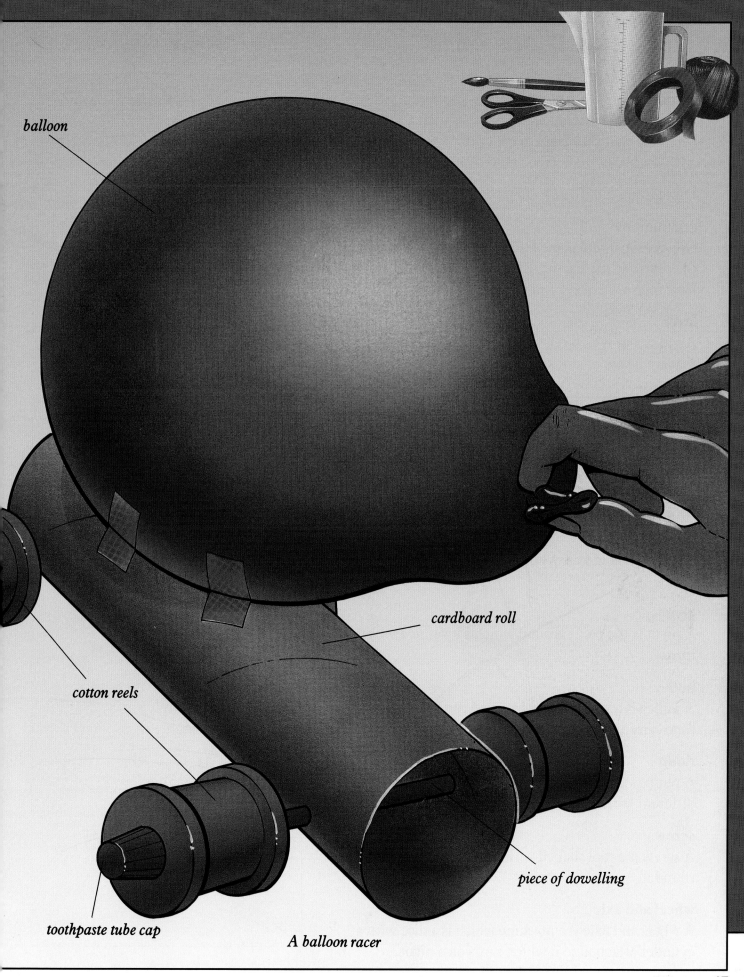

balloon

cotton reels

toothpaste tube cap

cardboard roll

piece of dowelling

A balloon racer

Glossary

apprentice
An apprentice is someone who works with a skilled person so that they can learn his job.

drive
Drive is to set or to keep a machine moving.

gravitational pull
Gravitational pull is the force that attracts things to the centre of the Earth. All stars, planets and moons have their own gravitational pull.

lever
A rod or bar which can be used to help lift objects that are heavy or stuck.

lift
Lift is the upward push of the air on the wings of birds and aeroplanes.

lubricate
To lubricate is to make surfaces slippery to reduce friction.

mason
A mason is someone who is skilled in working with stone.

pivot
A pivot is the point around which a lever or a wheel turns.

pulley
A pulley is a wheel with a grooved rim in which a rope can run to help lift something.

ramp
A ramp is a slope which connects two surfaces at different levels.

screw
A screw is a tool shaped with a spiral ridge running round it.

wheel and axle
A wheel and axle is a machine which is a disc with a cylinder attached to it which turns on a pivot.

Index

aerofoil 19
air 6, 18, 19, 28, 29
air pressure 16, 17
air resistance 8, 10, 12

belts 45
block and tackle 36, 37
boats 6
brakes 12, 13
braking distance 13

Cayley, George 24 – 27
Cody, Samuel 20
cogs 31, 44

flight 18 – 27
forces 4, 30
friction 14, 36

gearwheels 44
gliders 21, 22
gravity 5, 10

hovercraft 29

kites 20, 23

lever 31, 32, 40, 42
lift 18
Lilienthal, Otto 21

machines 30 – 33, 36

Newton, Isaac 5
newtons 5

parachutes 10, 12
pivot 31
pulleys 31, 32, 34 – 37, 40, 43

ramp 31, 32, 41

sails 6
screws 31, 32, 40
streamlined 8, 18

thermal 21
tools 32, 33

wheel and axle 31, 32, 35, 42
windmill 6, 7
wings 18, 19, 21
Wright, Orville and Wilbur 21